Also by Maurice Scully:

Poetry

Love Poems and Others (Raven Arts Press, 1981)
5 Freedoms of Movement (Galloping Dog Press, 1987)
Prior (Staple Diet, 1991; tel-let, 1992)
Certain Pages (Form Books, 1992)
Over and Through (Poetical Histories, 1992)
The Basic Colours (Pig Press, 1994)
Priority (Writers Forum, 1995)
Prelude, Interlude and *Postlude* (all Wild Honey Press, 1997)
Steps (Reality Street Editions, 1998)
Etruscan Reader IV
    (with Bob Cobbing & Carlyle Reedy: Etruscan Books, 1996, 1999)
5 Freedons of Movement (revised edition, Etruscan Books, 2001)
Tree with Eggs (hardPressed poetry, 2004)
Livelihood (Wild Honey Press, 2004)
Numbers (Coracle Press, 2006)
Sonata (Reality Street Editions, 2006)

CD
Mouthpuller (Wild Honey Press/Coelacanth Press, 2000)

Children's
What Is The Cat Looking At? (Faber, 1995)

MAURICE SCULLY

Tig

Shearsman Books
Exeter

Published in the United Kingdom in 2006 by
Shearsman Books Ltd
58 Velwell Road
Exeter EX4 4LD

ISBN-10   0-907562-96-5

ISBN-13   978-0-907562-96-2

Copyright © Maurice Scully, 2006.

The right of Maurice Scully to be identified as the author of this work has been asserted by him in accordance with the Copyrights, Designs and Patents Act of 1988. All rights reserved. No part of this publication may be reproduced, stored in a retrieval system, transmitted in any form or by any means, electronic, mechanical, photocopying, recording or otherwise, without the prior permission of the publisher.

Acknowledgements

Some parts of this book have appeared in *Angelaki*, *The Gig* & *Cyphers* & in the e-zines *Free Verse* & *Masthead*. Grateful thanks to the editors & all concerned.

The publisher gratefully acknowledges financial assistance from
Arts Council England.

Contents

Stepping	7
I.	
[Blessing the Animals]	11
II.	
[Backyard]	17
[Waterway]	20
[Backyard]	25
III.	
[A Falling Leaf]	33
[Picking Persimmon]	35
Coda	
[A Place to Stay]	43
Sonnet	46
Coda Coda	
Sonnet Ode: Blessing the Animals	51
Bread	59
I.	61
II.	67
III.	75
Coda	81
Coda Coda	93
[A Place. To Stay]	95
Notes	101

STEPPING

[BLESSING THE ANIMALS]

then
        the spring-born population stays put
in its region of birth
        the Great Lakes of North America.

then
        of the autumn-born population
⅓ hibernates
        while the remaining ⅔
set out southwards
        on a narrow unwavering route.
it's a journey of 3000 kilometres
        down to south Texas/northern Mexico.

on arrival they gather in one or two
        valleys on particular conifers
in their millions
        & rest there till spring
& mate.

then this immense blizzard of wings
        begins to move northwards
travelling in a more leisurely way
        feeding & laying their eggs along the route . . .

                the train's shadow
                flickering over the fields

the Monarch is a long-lived butterfly
        each individual surviving approximately
one year.
        their migration pattern is as follows

                        a child nearby
                        at a window

(migration pattern is as)

where the world
tracks past a

very young child
so happy so

taken aback
she

sings. (follows) & it beats
disclosing enclosing

flash! fold *flash!*
close slit show shock

blind shock black
shock/light exuding

over the visible
light intruding

on the visible
light corroding

the leaves leaving
only the light.

their

             dispersal   patterns

        are as   follows.

     map.   stop.

count.   then

        immense   upsurge

          white   red

                    amber   dark

the need for flattened bark-dwelling insects
to get away from predators on tree-trunks may
well have provided the selective pressure that
led to the evolution of wings – between rains
we lay listening lay waiting – you know me . . .

   rain on glass to the side of yr face

```
┌─────────────────────────────────┐
│                                 │
│                                 │
│                                 │
│                                 │
└─────────────────────────────────┘
```

   a door shut in a corridor

[BACKYARD]

so that.

      when the
            leaves
                  stiffen
                        flare
disconnect

& quietly
        fall detached from
their place at

each point (exact) landing in even
circles anding at different
times the

     different

on flat green grass & (echo – tussled hair –
handshake) litter   collect
that

different (or) touching a windowpane where
drops gather ( ) difference ( ) &
or different

( ) colours even. stopped outside a fruitshop
on a corner
warmer

than December remember hands
pink that weigh/&/
gilt scales

splinters of pieces of vivid
boxes shelves
fruitsmell

in passing talking to I was
talking to
you were

saying quick/shadow-flash
(pigeons) quick
past

sunlit walls then (pattern)
then gone/look.
what?

stunned/back from hospital
on the way back too
back to the wall

my old dead
father in
shadow

in the Shadow of
hearing for
sure

its articul
ate whis
per |

core to granulated
crust my
dull

moves & days/
thunder-
clashes

& a train overhead.
it is porous
&

dangerous it is
porous/it is
pour it.

[WATERWAY]

   suddenly
yr tomb a little
block of stone
placed fast to
   the spot

  yr name
       gone
not
       suddenly
sudden
       ly
yes
       gone
gone
       traces
to be
       sure but
gone
       vanished
into
       air
take it
       to where
you will
       but
cut
       where's
my
       map?
where's
       my
hammer
       gone?
who
       said

goodbye
    &/from
one side
    here
not wide
    fly
true
    to
the other
    but
  deaf
  frail
  blind
step & then
    a step
       (gone)
reading out
    reading out
the signs
    for you
in the park
    loud
step
    & then a
step
    ash
flame
    holly
yellow
    & bloated
in the
    end
the
    drugs
(step)
    given you
oh to
    help you

to help
        you yes
the packet
        says
Lethe
        or
Lever
        or
Leave It
        can you
hear it?
        from one
little
        drug
company
        to
another
        with
love
        a sort
of circ-
        ulating
siren-
        echo
quietly
        stitched
in
        to
that
        logo
that
        gets
round
        to
help
        you
(ste/p)
        yes

    leave
          now
    but
          suddenly
    to
          grieve
    what's
          that?
    let's
          argue
    (gone)
          where's
    my biro?
          my note-
    pad?
          what date's
    today?
          is it
    raining?
          my news-
    paper?
          shoes?
    dog?
          tell me
    tell me

      colour pictures
            moving snaps
slipping channels
          shadows
          &
    quietness
          &
          fathers
   whirl
        about
  a name
  is probably a

definite article
in somebody's
statute in sub-
terranean heaven
somewhere but
here
      a blank.

   step &
      then a
   step.

[BACKYARD]

v-ripples echoing
action underwater
sing amor for shelter
forever from sharks

in that dark welter
of trouble-dogging-
the-innocent in this
Holding Centre for

Continuing Re-education
curiously thought to
consist – down to the
root Lie of the Land –

Life. gulls sparrows
bees feeding a heron
a cat spider in wait
brittle reflections

on still pools oakleaf
folded in a muddy crevice
my left hand to my right
quick blur my fingers

my way of life. how does
god remember all the
things in the right place
of us? how does he stick

them on? are we just
photographs talking (I
put the daisy wheel
in its box) or what? my

daughter (4). name
on a plate on a door.
tree-sure treasure
a small spider quiet

in a corner covering
for a time what appears
there moving – glory! –
& spectacular sensations

developing under the
tongue. well now turn-
ing over the papyrus
here it strikes us

one life one elong-
ated crisis (with
modulations) icy
fingers of discomfort

in the lower back each
stiff hair to its nerve-
cell (notify yr solicitor
when that picket of *ifs*

cuts across yr precious
precarious spinney) alert
& ready: "comfort" is

    wrong. yes?

        &
        a song
        shh
        is
        I was told

```
                    stack
                    blade
                    bit

                    is
                    *work*

                    work?

shaving the white wood smooth in the shadows

quite    thank you for that

a wave
          collapsing on its patch of sand

                    a
                      fresh
                    a
                      is

not so very long ago
                         quietly one Saturday
morning
        detached

            one piece of old hat
            deserves another
            after all

                    whittle
                    gouge
                    stop

                    *work*
                    they said
```

      a song
      they said
      note
          don't
      do you?
      a

      sh
      ap
      e.
      ah.

out of the
chequerwork
barbed dazzle
of Difficulty-

in-Life suddenly
I espied me a
gap in the defences
& Light's

eager
molecular chain
in frenzy just
without. an ABC

turn it
over look in
peer down dizzy
to find (then

crossing the
mountains we
got stranded
one night) –

high gloss low
visibility – in
the undancing face
of a boulder in yr

path:

Calculated Greed.

fat stem.
tiny branches.
enormous yellow flowers.

too short too partisan too frag
mented too unintelligible the
issue too difficult to decypher
who's who in this & what is it any-

way an accelerating bubble on a swollen
tide – machines of war memory perception –
whose meanings can't any more be pre-
figured or absorbed cultures inverted

to prey on not "cradle" "civilizations"
lulling or eliminating peoples for the
use of a few invisible manipulators of
no country or allegiance – theft –

parasitic on a scale never before thought
possible to succeed – eating up humanity.
eating it up. meanwhile old-world lyrics
get prizes in small quaint corners. &

good luck to them. *An Ceangal:* in this
particular out-building to the Forgotten
Gaelic Tradition I find the Blackbird of
Anywhere-At-All quite likely to be in two

minds on one branch. leaf-swish. between the dictionary & the air-shapes, the intermission. try harder. bigger vistas, less credulity. *cementery* is good. yes?

    sing Amor.

III

[A FALLING LEAF]

cryptic snippets in yr pockets
by some loose change on the floor
lie quiet as you lie with her
yr day's dazed thoughts on buses
libraries the street.

it's supposed to add up to something
& be greater than the sum of its parts
too not statistics through the window you're
always gazing graphs & diagrams of the heart
without scale or co-ordinates
unlike the "simplicities of nature"
or many aspects of a discipline
presuming to think you know
the mind ready & the scene set.

.

people have to expect to be seen
to expect to be believed
innocent of bureaucracy
insistent the tune
slips through level or not.

people can be born to expect to be loved
not conned insist to be
the source out of which
the music issues level irregular
November   October   anywhere.

things written between
things selected things new
& collected things &   so on.
a business of. & filing.
can conned people expect understanding?

.

orbiting around the great liquid spine of the river

                                                older

salmon & sea trout in & out of the worlds of
salt & fresh water

older

rarest plant   purple milk vetch   low-growing perennial
whimbrel & tufted frunnock
fruit an elongated hairy pod

                   older

I took my children to the sea
              the dog barked

    they build sandcastles
I built castles we had
3 then 9
    castles
poisoning
    watched planes arrive

suddenly

older

[PICKING PERSIMMON]

distinctly through
the night air trains

through otherwise
silence – contact –

toy-like parallel
movements where machinery

clocks into place.
listen I saw what

I meant you saw
& the sunny external

world slid past over
yr shaded spectacles

& for the sake of
the rhythm I suppose

of the train on its
track you smiled.

it all takes you back.

under an intimate
intense cone of light

on a page on a desk
among books in the night

to return upturn upset
visit obsessive hating

obsessed teaching the
cocky ignorant well-to-do

offspring of the European
upper echelons to

limp along in something
like an intelligible

legible *béarlagar*
tax free on the button . . .

I always liked being there
that dark & haunting house

off the South Circular
at the canal end where

colossal mirrors
spread out their

cloth ducks in flight
across a wall

oranges & lemons
& the bells

of St Clement's &
the strangeness

of flickering eyes
that are blind –

oh movements
continuous &

formal forgive
us our futures!

& loneliness.
& affection

that atom
incandescent

in the tune
the train's

shadow flickering
over the fields

mountains passing
(a city, distant)

gull-spots wheeling

a child nearby
at the window

where the world
tracks past a

very young child
so happy so

taken aback
she sings . . .

                                                                                                                   & farre

                                                                                                                                                                   exelle

                                                                        all other strowing

                                                                                                                           herbes

                        for to decke up houses

                                                                                                                                                                    slate

web

                     clay

                                  weed

pebbles

             withered root

                                                            dust

                                                                                      litter

           spider

                    flicker of leaves lodged at the stub

            a tree

        is a multiparticular planar miracle

is a book   an electronic blur   a minúte variation hook

   is a door   a still   my notes   hats   quotes

   the shadows moving in the breeze in the sunlight
beside the white house outside the village by the sea

               change

---

     found a nest
     in a hedge

     its centre a
   weave of hair
from the family's
       dog

silky oval precise
ly birdbody-size
no egg   some plastic
      string.

CODA

[A PLACE TO STAY]

Go little thing   be good
black thread   spicule   white
solid radiant basis
carved cradled care-driven materials
twisting the texture
to him who has his senses still
baaah! goes the train on the line
yes & twisting she moves
& still – to balance –
arthritic & pert places in the spine
that plain stab-of-the-beak
& twist – *baaah!* – chance – a hand –
step – spread in the light –
see shade you don't dread
thread where you are a long
time-thing radiant
bright cone – *baaah!* – too –
not a word –
dough lolly loot
dough lolly loot.
good.

   .

Profile to phonepiece
edged by light
a tenseness in the silence of the room
in the time it takes
catching a tangle of cables
the sun beyond the window
takes   it takes to &
the time it takes to
find out   is it
is it
really alright?

   .

Nets in flight in the half-light
& has his senses still
& sense & has stillness
& sense
start up the stairs again
as early as you can

   there can be no very
to carry yr cares
   there can be no very
to pen the tune
   there can be no very
black melancholy
to him who
hurry
let's hurry across to the island
to see the notetaker
       soulmaker
         soulmate . . .

   woke   here is the
   nine o'clock   in the
   temperate zones   when
   I   you said to me

   I see (nine) reading
   my   quiet have I not
   been (news) thinking
   of you were there are

      some gaps here.

Assembly of hounds

Otherworldly sustenance

Shelter of the wounded

Power of the weak

Dregs of clothing

Most noble goodliness

SONNET

quietly   more quietly go
playfully   accept
except

———————————————

quietly
       more quietly still
smiling

———————————————

she left a leaf on my desk

———————————————

it fell

———————————————

tree-bit

———————————————

down. (earth)
       that.
land on it.
     ignition

———————————————

the word for *quick*
in this language

a dog at a door
barricade

———————————————

blackback tilts & turns
robin under privet

———————————————

what a zero glass cube
to write up

---

plant a little seed
in the big black earth

---

wait

---

a fly stopped on a stone
grooming

---

hare　　　*giddy person*

　　　　　　　　otter　　　*water snake*

retaliate　　*demons*

　　　　　　　　tor　　*belly*

vanquish　　*and*

　　　　　　　　weel　*use*

whisper　　*synonymous*

　　　　　　　　zone　*colour*

zymurgy　　*maker of leaven*

---

she left a leaf on my desk

CODA CODA

SONNET ODE: BLESSING THE ANIMALS

ONE

    that tendency
    & I see towards
    bisymmetry

                        until she was 49 & then
                        only because she found a
                        canvas her sister had left behind

    like a hand of
    a clock an egg
    I'll

                        Things Are Ready
                        or Answering Laughter or
                        Are You Passing

    kid pops through porch
    glancing
        slips away
        laughs

                        A Title is another &
                        Titled & then: White
                        Balloon Hidden

    moving over hills
    in silent ripples
    wild brushwork
            colour-intricacies
    ten then see

        [crystals & grids]

                        & then a slat gave way
                        & you slipped & fell
                        into

    the boiling sea (one-two)
    between the ship & the quay
    (two-three)

                      & yr World or Clique [h'mm
                      haven't decided that one yet]
                      tightens to set tò

    amid gambits   crypto-babble
       paper clips   staples
    books   papers

                      the flickering shadows
                      of career commentators
                      & their recent acquisitions

    among the strangler
    fig. snow. a quick
    wind bangs

                      the roof. a slab hits
                      the skylight.

    jet-line through
    cloud-spot/water-flash/
    sea-flash/

                      electrical fizzle
                      between communicating
                      pairs

            how proud we are

            how proud of you
                we are

              how very
              very

              ART

Bread
has been
an important
food

ever since man
first learned how to grind
cereals into flour.

The
earliest
loaves
were simple unleavened cakes

dried in the sun.

Leavened bread is mentioned
in the earliest chapters
of the Bible
& seems to have been invented
by the Egyptians.

Splendid & unforgettable are the shrines of the gods

How fine they look in their ancient groves

Splendid the Gods

how fine they look

set round with the Jewel Fence

an unworldly air

Splendid & unforgettable are the shrines of the gods.
How fine they look in their groves of ancient trees
that wear an unworldly air, set round with the jewel fence
& on the sacred saka tree the white cloth symbol hung.

TWO

How do you do.
Tundish.
Thanks.

le seinm na gcuach ar bhruach
na gcoille go sámh.
O Hope

spread wide your Narrow Hands!

He dropped in   unexpectedly too
had tea (tay)
        2 sugars   black.
                Steam.

Strange faces reflected upside-down
in the liquid in my cup
the other day.
        (Séamas Dall)

It's an ABC turn it over
look in peer
    down dizzy
        to find

(then crossing the mountains we got stranded one night)

one drunk woman
        far
          below sway. In the
present. Pattern. BC.

    Moving over old photographs of Avoca
    wistful of the past not that not
    certainly not falls

on a map a timetable a list one egg
two impromptus &
a mark.

Picking persimmon by the waterway
with the health officer
of the brigade.

They loved music vine-spiralling the
trellis she loved the
trellis

he the cross-sections. Avocation. And
regret. Next please. Down. Thank
you.

    I
   dig
  & I-my
   tater
   digs
  & his-his
   tad-tad
   tug
   too
   ho-hum
   swet
   wet
   slap
   coily
   oily
 & splasht it
   yep
   said
 good ah good
   slippy
   man
   said

                    dug
                every body
                    said
                   yep-yep
                    petty
                  gun-squat
                   yup that
                     sit
                    dug
                what a pin is
                    what
                    uhm
                    lout
                    what
                un/derlocking
                    tatty
                    hoker
                     yap
                     yap
                    snappy
                            bang
                                of
                                  the
                                        boots
                                  of
                                  the
                   obvious
                    bang
                    bang
                 tap dizzy ah
                  daddy oh
                    dug
                 little brittles
                   with a
                   new skin
                    cheap
                     tap
                     tap

good
good

Natives were capturing guns runs the narrative while
bad lads in their labs dally as mere
ballads dandle the baby-culture

& slaps together on the sharps: at 52/104
I've had quite enough
Creativity

      Free Expression, Genius & all that.
      Quits.

      Let's communicate.

And entered a private street. Footsteps stretch. As this, then
that. Tick/tock. Predatory plumage, & the pen I write with
combine on the one vine – let it rain, let it rain – so that
by half-past ten I entered the train with my ticket, playing
musical instruments. Then gold, then red from a rainbow
around our heads (how many anniversaries/how many
pebbles make a path out?) the sky shot through with eyes
looking up.

More & more this gets on yr nerves (black slab over the bay,
porcelain gull-dots that tilt & disappear) until voices: *Ah-ha
then Mr Recluse, what's in yr pockets, eh?* Ghost-diktats, paper,
gold reserves.

BREAD

A sack of white flour fell off a lorry outside a funeral parlour. There was a funeral in progress. It was raining and the flour congealed and became slippy. A man with a haversack on his back crossing the road stepped on a patch of the porridgy mess . . .

Whorls of branchlets swept and trailing to the water's rhythm, the female can be seen as a green oval flask-shaped surprise, the male spherical orange sculpted exterior that breaks into eight sections in maturity releasing clouds . . .

Throwing himself to the side of an on-coming van and into a cyclist's path, the front wheel jams in a drain, the cyclist lands on the bonnet of the van, his bicycle topples onto a dog sniffing a wet stain on the back tyre of a hearse, the van hits a bollard, the cyclist slides off, the haversack-carrier rolls to safety, an old lady looks round, the funeral's fiscal graphline rose, the sets were perfect, the lead got up.

The hearse driver looked round. The van driver got out. The bus stopped. Traffic lights changed red. A goods train trundled by on a bridge overhead: black/orange, black/orange, black. Frequency times length equals velocity. Hello? Yes? Splendid! It's a quarter past three, mid-point in the wave . . .

essen	in part
tiall	by grou
y a p	pings o
oem i	f twent
s a f	y-six q
lat s	uite we
urfac	ll-know
e cov	n-symbo
ered	ols.

As to each delicate item in the hive yr trivia is as engaging as my trivia. And sticks. Then palps to the paralysed hymenoptera: busy busy busy.

or:

a
song
is
a

a
song
is
a

a
song
is
a

sh
ap
e

SONNET

From the nine facts the typist is
Charlotte & the nurse must be Alice.
The hostess lives west of Charlotte &
Doris lives directly north of the typist.
Therefore Doris can't be the hostess.
Putting the results into a small map
it will turn out that Alice lives
four miles south & three miles west of Doris
which by Pythagoras makes the distance
five miles. And Betty, of course, is the hostess.

11

I feel I should feel better now.
Here you will feel better later.
Later   later   even later.
Better later.

wall couple

coop.

    don't eat sweets
    don't pick your nose
    don't piss in yr knickers
                  – the beginning.

&
a
song
is
I was told
shh

stock
blade
bit

shaving the white wood smooth in the shadows

step

quite   thank you for that

clouding the egg that develops then
into a dark thick-walled spore

a
  fresh
a
  is
they
  said

not (what?) not so long ago
                            one quiet Saturday
afternoon
      detached

nick
whittle
gouge

a song
they said

note
      don't
do you?
a

sh
ap
e
ah

yes

falling

earth return
earthshine
ear trumpet
earwax
earwig
ease

hammer that home & sell it.

happy art fluid art
who are so
serious

happy art a cow
in experience
daisies

buttercup grass happy
art a vow to
experience

stems earth god's little cow
a bright enamel dot
ambling over

grasses & tested in
the root of yr
fly zoom

e-sus in the sky nested in
for once. happy
art.

sit up. take stock. a leaf
in life rayed
luminous

& glinting in a slight
breeze until
the –

rolling barely over oblong
stain for us inwards
now

& at the power of our breath
again – until
the

until the
until the
Descent to Earth

Quick, turn, disappear under a sliding keel, return, silver, gold-black, green, slipping into many waters many times once on one rival map after another, twining –

step –

the fish rise. Bank to bank. Unravel. Arrive. *YA!* goes the storm in the trees. *YA!* The violins are working hard now. [*YA!*] Is that broken stone down there your oh your *heart?* Life, one backlit bedchamber after another connected by feather-lined corridors in a ring . . . Phone me when you get back.

    cutting

    or vibrating

    or light arriving

    snapping into place

    multiple as seeds
       in tight array

    like burning firewood

    leaves dispersing

    visiting strangers

    a dry mudball

    mixing lacquer

    spring water welling up

pulse

  like dusty earth

  like being stopped by a horizontal partition

  like a suspended curtain
  black

  like a sword lying flat
   about to be gripped

  like that

  like a smooth pill

  like glory . . .

beats a rhythm in the dust

 pelvis swaying
 look like this
  away to
  from to
 shatters &
 re-forms
 it matters & it gathers

 fingertips to the
 (*Nei Ching*)
 of the many links
 so many
 of the many links
 that make up the twisted chain

 in love
 the twisted chain
 "detail
  is all."
   In hate:
 orchestration.

    but "carry the message"

                    a fat ark under a tree
                    & the agua rising

who signed
what for whom?
what?   when?

              in 1803 Hicks & his growing
              family

the Holy Spirit

              & the Metropolitan Museum of Art
              in New York

alterations &
touches

              a sleepy little village in Ireland
              then Ennis for godsake after Ha Tulo

under a bluegum tree
        swish & glisten
        not human sacrifice after all for a minute but
not to limit
yrself to Peaceable Kingdom paintings

                    too/either

        ok then:
        carry one

    the tendency
    & I see towards
    bisymmetry

                        until she was 49 & then
                        only because she found a
                        canvas her sister had left

    behind like the hand of
    a clock an egg
    I'll

                        Things Are Ready
                        or Answering Laughter or
                        Are You Passing

    kid pops through porch
    glancing
            slips away
                laughs

                        hello ellen. hello helen.
                        have you heard? there's
                        been a horrible accident.

    oh dear. what's happened?
    hilda higgins' husband
    has had an accident

                        on his horse. how awful!
                        is he injured? how did
                        it happen?

    A Title is another &
    Titled & then: White
    Balloon Hidden

        note wild brushwork
        very wristy
                ten then see

crystals & grids

---

        drop stops & the tops
        will crop for themselves

that's five

    I mean tip

        wonderful   may be

        it's a game in hide & seek
        or dip & pursuit/quite formal/
        too   see/saw

six

    said

        sad at supper
        happy by midmorning through
        the following week
        briefly

        spark

BUT/
    in about 1841 for reasons
    so far undiscovered Field
    & his wife, & daughter Henriette,
    moved to New York City

        I'll never now grow up to be
        "an illustrious itinerant limner
        with a bustling career"

flower flowing

        neat in the ell of my trim lapel

CODA

a wisp of smoke from a village on a hilltop

a spider from a lamp

a bird saws   over & over   law-seem   daw-son   drop!

an apple   an egg

black points. gold stars. oily inside upper of a buttercup.

he just came in & sang some songs.

But what a price the Japanese women paid.

one such engraved amulet made of onyx presented to St Alban's Abbey by Aethelred the Unready

In the early days of broadcasting the BBC Advisory Committee on Spoken English helped those "whose daily duty it is to broadcast the world's news"

Scraping Bird   Bird-Twang   Squeak   Fiddle   flit from black to black

gaps   hollows   ridges   organized spaces

But what/this noise, what is it?

Did he say: it's yr mind   or it's *in* yr mind?

This is the first time I (see this film)

In medieval Denmark the custom of tying the skin of a white worm round the waist of the parturient woman prevailed.

to wake up

& resting . . . to wake up, without echo, step by step, the green domes, gull on a flagpole, in the first place & stop . . . but what/ this noise, what is it?

Echo says: you.

> Then it's true?
> Eyes get colder
> & that changes
>
> the luminous
> instant/cut/
> Bolder sd
>
> Ominous
>
> but does it? the sun
> caught on rooftops
> delays us
>
> a silver dot
> in the sky
> making a bright white
>
> line
>
> too a noise
> stormslapped flag
> (& its absence:
>
> gull on a stone)
> pebbles that click on a wave's recession
> over a beach
>
> then . . .
>
> So it's true?

Japanese women are not likely to bang a shoe on the table.

All that these able writers have said on language has been challenging, provocative, & generally very helpful.

Thank you.

                        clutching a bright
                                    blur of fruit
                  your mother gave you
                                    you disappear into
            childhood
                                    over a metal bridge
            & on to a train
                        for school forever.
                                    tact.
                  the ceremony begins.
                              black into white
                              & back.
      butterflies erupt & disappear over a hedge.
                                    seeds on a single gust
            across the neighbourhood
                                    you circle thus/quick
      where's your pencil?
                        is that a map?
                  sails, distant.
                              cliffbase. flecks.
                  oily movements
                        in a pear-shaped stone.
                        burst of rain on the roof overhead.
                  that blunt instrument
                                    yr mind.
                  the ceremony begins
                        it all begins
                  all of it
                        all begins
                        over again
                        to
                        travel up to
                              let the eye travel
                        slowly
                        up the stem
                  green
                        up along it
                        in a pocket of light
                        leaves
                        light cilia
                        to the shaped
                        silver in the air
                        then
                              to the flowers
                  moving &
                        the leaves
                        & the light in them
                              up
                        inhale it
                  pass
                  green
                  blue
                  red

then
long branching
stems
with whorls
of branchlets
swept
& trailing
to the
water's
pulse
the female
can be seen
as a green
oval flask-shaped
surprise
    the male
    spherical
    orange
    chiselled exterior
    that breaks into eight
    intricate sections
    in maturity
    releasing clouds . . .
        clouding
        the egg that
        develops then
        into a
        dark
        thick-walled
        spore
        which falls
        from the plant
        giving
        rise
        in the end
        to a
        new
        startle of

long
thin
branching
stems
that are splendid
        splendid & unforgettable

grasp sparrow's tail
        single whip
play guitar
        lean forward
picking persimmon
        in the backyard
by the waterway
        blessing the animals
without panic
        white crane
spreads its
        wings
brush knee & twist
        step
brush knee & fix
        step
step forward
        to the waterway
with the health
        officer of the brigade
small intricate
        sounds   bread
descent to earth
        a falling leaf
migrating butterflies
        white balloon hidden

grasp sparrow's tail
        single whip
play guitar
        lean forward
white crane
        spreads its wings
brush knee
        & twist –
step –
        play guitar
brush knee

          & fix – step –
step forward
        deflect
downward
        intercept &
punch
        draw back

(split) & push

windshield wipers
        a pale finger
on cold glass
        in the rain
dusty steel
        grainy wash
bubbles in a
        bathtub
the clouds in
        patterns
the winds
        the leaves
day/night
        spinning &
dissolving
        trickling
down to
        roots whose
roots
        have roots
& connect
        in a vivid
zigzag of
        changing
agreements
        in a glaze
below
        the surface

    you lately
           reached through
  to.
          touched.
  but . . .

dandelion & daisy

cross hands

dandelion & daisy begin

cross hands

cross hands folding.

Beginning of an answer

Beginning of calling

Beginning of slaying

Sustenance of bees

Beauty of eyebrows

Lustre of eye-light

Beginning of honey

CODA CODA

[A PLACE.
TO STAY]

tools made from
bric-a-brac this
& that the river
gave up

you were ending
your circle a
littered track
of extravagant

things a tiny
garden at the back
run wild a neat
platform set in

the fork of a
sycamore over a
stream to sink
the water bucket

in your face in
the sky as you
dreamed the mild
losing interlock

of the made with
the growing put
through your wry
smile dreaming . . .

tishhh go cars on
wet streets filter-
ing yellow through
dense scaffolding

casting black on
black from rainwind

in waves outside –
shadowy – midnight –

mind your head –
place your foot –
who's there?

one night on
the roof watching
the scattered

light-sparkle on the
hills around the city
my boot cracked open a

sheet of pale blue
polystyrene to fall
suddenly through
the dark but: pulled

back. stopped short:
    terrified.

    then.

migrating butterflies

blessing the animals

picking persimmon

bit by bit/the whole
spread rising structure
wooden arcs spiral
staircase ornate clock.

    the ant
    moves the
    grain.

                    then left out
                            refuse
            head touched canopy
                            clouds of greenfly
        nodded to
                neighbours
                            stepped in back
                                        for more bags
        slight discomfort in the left
                        foot (Tuesday)
    bus goes by
                            dog slips in
                pushed handle
                            down through the hallway
                then turned to close
                            the

                    otherwise/
                    Migrating
                    Butterflies
                    Blessing the
                    Animals Picking
                    Persimmon A
                    Falling Leaf
                    /// Descent
                    to Earth Panic
                    Backyard A
                    Sparrow A
                    Title Tig Bread
                    White Balloon
                    Hidden Health
                    Officer of the
                    Brigade   Cockfight
                    Waterway   A Place to
                Stay   Always   Always

Dandelion & daisy begin.

Soon the sweetish whiff

of wallflower & walks

past the Ashtown Tin Box Factory

down to the pouring canal.

Notes

"anding" on p17 is not a misprint, the "tufted frunnock" [p34] not a bird.

The Irish Language

Tig, house [English sense intended also].

An Ceangal [p29] *L'envoi.*

béarlagar [p36] jargon, from *béalra:* "mouth rubbish" which in turn gives us *Béarla,* the Irish word for the English language.

le seinm na gcuach ar bhruach na gcoille go sámh [p54] "with the cuckoo's peaceful singing on the edge of the wood" (Séamas Dall MacCuarta, 1650? – 1733)

bóin dé, a ladybird, "God's little cow" [p72]

Briatharogham: pp45 & 92 (closing 6 & 7 lines respectively). These are cryptic two-word glosses on ogham letter-names found in medieval mss, but much older than this and meant to be mnemonic. They are oblique, obscure and undependable. And extraordinary.

Tig is the closing volume of *Things That Happen* which comprises:

1:      *5 Freedoms of Movement*

2:      *Livelihood*
                — *The Basic Colours*
                — *Zulu Dynamite*
                — *Priority*
                — *Steps*
                — *Adherence*

---

3 :   *Sonata*

Coda: *Tig*

1981 – 2006

www.ingramcontent.com/pod-product-compliance
Lightning Source LLC
Chambersburg PA
CBHW032057150426
43194CB00006B/565